Sidney Wade

Bird Book

Sidney Wade's poetry has appeared in *The Best American Poetry, The New Yorker, The Nation, Poetry Magazine,* and many other publications. She is the author of six previous volumes of poems: *Straits & Narrows, Stroke, Celestial Bodies, Empty Sleeves, Green,* and *From Istanbul.* A Fulbright scholar and translator, Wade has served as president of the Association of Writers & Writing Programs (AWP) and is Professor Emerita at the University of Florida, where she taught creative writing and served as poetry editor for the literary journal *Subtropics.*

SidneyWade.com

Bird Book

poems

for Cindy
thanks for listening!
Happy Birding!

Sidney Wade

ATELIER26 BOOKS
Portland, OR

Cover design and image layout by Nathan Shields
Book design by M.A.C.

Interior images by John James Audubon,
courtesy of audubon.org/birds-of-america

Bird Book
(poetry)
isbn-13: 978-0-9976523-3-8
isbn-10: 0997652330

Library of Congress Control Number:
2017942676

Atelier26 Books are printed in the U.S.A. on acid-free paper

ATELIER26 BOOKS, an independent publisher in
Portland, Oregon, exists to demonstrate the
powers and possibilities of literature through
beautifully designed and expressive books that
Atelier26   get people listening, talking, and exchanging
ideas.

Distributor: Small Press United/Independent Publishers Group
(IPG)

The valued support of Tina Alonso helped make this book
possible.

Atelier26 is grateful for grant support from the Oregon
Community Foundation.

Atelier26Books.com

For the Birds

And for Amanda, Elena, and Woodie

Love

Contents

*

First green flare / 11
A bird / 12
Burrowing Owl / 14
Birds / 16
Indigo Bunting / 18
Marsh Poodle / 20
Red-winged Blackbirds in the Rain / 24
Cardinal / 26
Killdeer Bathing / 28
The Great White Pelican / 30
Interlude / 34
The Wide-eyed Vireo / 36
Whimbrel / 38
Snow Bird / 40
Bejeweled / 42
Turkey Vultures / 43
Glory Train / 46
The Chickasaw Trees / 50
Bird and Beast / 54
Birding at the Hamilton County
              Phosphate Mines / 55
The Truth About Cats / 58
Snowy Owl / 61
Swan Lake / 63
Sparrowing / 66
Bird Words / 68
Blue / 71
Osprey and Needlefish / 73

Loon / 76

Black-bellied Whistling Ducks / 78

What Rough Beast / 81

Birding at the Dairy / 83

King Vulture / 86

Thirty white / 88

Amazed / 89

Dry Season / 93

Witness Tree Junction,
        Rochelle, FL / 95

*

The Hard Saving / 97

Acknowledgments / 100

BirdBook

First green flare

makes
the air

quiver
and dart

the throat
ache

to call
makes

the heart
cheer

the ear
keen

to the sheer
glorious

windfall
of oriole

veery
vireo

A bird

is a word
abroad

in air
on a stem

with roots
a gem

in scarlet
lemon

brown
the fruit

of import
from above

a weather
report

in short
a swift noun

a small
requiem

for all
that passes —

love
wind

grasses

Burrowing Owl

Very odd,
this little cloud

in trousers
in the sandy

fortress
favored by

prairie dog
and gopher

tortoise.
On the mound

at the mouth-hole,
he scouts around

with sybilline
yellow eyes

and then, owl-
wise, decides

to clean house.
He dives down

and soon
great clouds

of smudge come
flying out,

his home now
clean as a bone.

A diurnal owl,
he's upside-down

and inside-out,
at ease

not in trees,
but underground,

where his mate
broods

on her eight
fragile moons

in an immaculate
burrow whose

contours are lined
with cow manure.

Birds

are made
mostly of air.

They bear
scant weight

and many bright
colors. Eschewing

the freight
of matrimony,

they rarely mate
for life.

They lay
their speckled

eggs on stony
cliffs, on sea-wrack

or bare sand,
and in the grass.

Glass, alas,
often breaks

their necks
as they migrate

at night,
or in the bright

betrayals
of sunlight.

Indigo Bunting

blue as paint
blue as flame

blue as blue dawn
blue as the burn

after lightning
blue on fire

blue and a black beak
blue on electric wire

blue as the sky
just after dark

blue on the back
of the eye

blue as sleep
blue as a skyblue

dancer no bluer
blue as a sunning shark

blue as Nolde's
watercolor

blue shot
blue bead

bluer than the deep
indigo sea

blue as speed
blue fizz

blue black blue
dart and sizzle

Marsh Poodle

Absurd,
this watermark

shore-bird
who rackets

about, barking
like a yappy

poodle.
The black-

necked stilt
picks at

its food
with a needle-

thin bill
in knee-

deep water
as it hunts

by sight
for brine flies

and snails.
Long and

slender legs,
divinely

pink, trail
way behind

in flight.
You'd think

the stilt
was built

for speed,
but no,

it's pedigreed
in wading.

It saunters, or,
funnily, runs,

sprinkling
its way through

the shallows,
knees and ankles

bent backward
in liquid angles.

The truth is,
in its striking

and elegant
black and

white suit,
it's oddly

godly, and
beautiful

to the core,
as it bruits

about, spangling
the shore

Red-winged Blackbirds in the Rain

for Lizzie

Glossy
black

males
unpack

red
epaulettes

and sway
atop

wet
cattail

stems.
They

sing
conk-

a-reee
with

a tinny
buzz

just as
a dial-up

modem
does.

Cardinal

His head
isn't red,

it's black
as a scalded

sinner.
He's bald

and pitiful,
but brave,

as he picks
at his seeds

from the eminence
of the feeder,

a shaved
and wincing

avian prince
at his dinner.

What turns
a song-bird

vulturine?
cap too tight?

territorial fight?
a terrible flaw

in the grand design?
A cuckoo pope?

Nope.
Feather mites.

Killdeer Bathing

Distinctive
black collars

invisible,
he wriggles,

frisky,
in the drink.

He prinks
and sprinkles

dizzy
droplets

everywhere
in the morning

air. Restored,
he resumes

his chores —
the brisk

and worried
survey

of the shore,
the skitter,

feint,
and twist

of the natural
catastrophist.

The Great White Pelican

is dying.
The lake

in which
he slowly dies

is moribund
as well.

For days
now, he

has paddled
in circles

in the shallows,
his great elbows

lifted as if
to catch

a breeze.
It appears

he cannot feed
or fly and so

he'll starve
to death.

It's very slow.
Day by day,

the water lowers.
The mud brown

shore grows
by a breath

every twelve
hours.

The green
platters

of the lily pads
lie on ground

already fuzzed
with young weeds.

Yellow blossoms
grow straight

out of the drying
surface scum.

Pickerelweed
is stunted,

yet still,
pathetically,

blooms.
Where boats

once docked,
dog fennel

plumes
shoulder-high.

The blowzy
new land

bloats
up a mile

down to
the shrinking

fundament
of water,

its sediments
exhumed,

rheumy, dark,
and fecund.

Interlude

the never-ending
meditation

continues in
this early

morning
squirrels on

the porch
and in the trees

the lake is still
the silence

blue I've belled
the cat made

coffee and
am ready

with my pencil
to accept

whatever
mind imagines

is its music
or its body

or its gold
I've hung

the niger
thistle-seed

and am
waiting

for the cloud
of goldfinches

I hear is near
to appear.

The Wide-eyed Vireo

is grizzly
in hue.

His legs
are blue.

He fizzes
in witch-

hazel
and dizzy

thickets
of willow.

A secretive
and shrubby

dude,
he mimics

the tunes
of other birds,

though he
often repeats

his own
singular

words.
He feasts

on littler
beasts

he finds
with his yellow-

spectacled
wide-open eyes,

which he also
keeps peeled

(he's an avian
masher)

for a chance
encounter

with the double-
breasted

mattress
thrasher.

Whimbrel

Kin to
the limpkin,

she whimpers
when primping,

wears rimless
eyeglasses

for skimming
her primer

on swimming.
She splashes

through grasses
amassing

her rations
of shrimp,

and stands,
a fat ampersand,

on the sandpaper
strand

making eyes
at a snipe,

fanning
the passions

of the sandpiper
nation.

Snow Bird

I'm torn,
my beloved

in the ice-
ribbed north,

while here
in the sun

I feather
in the first

flush of green,
in the dazzle

of liquid return
to gold branches,

everything throbbing
with pollen

and birds, as
my love, amid

the swirling
snow words

of another storm,
bends his tired

back and shovels
some more.

Bejeweled

Corvus Marinus

The cormorant
(the water crow)

rises from below
where he stormed

through a swarm
of minnows

and lifts his head
and turns just so

sunlight bejewels
his radiant

eye-ringing
sapphires,

scintillating
marine

and corvine
bling.

Turkey Vultures

lack a syrinx,
so cannot sing.

They really stink.
Their red heads

are featherless
for cleanliness.

They have three sets
of eyelashes.

They wash
their pinkish

legs in rivulets
of urine,

which stain
them white

and cool
them down.

They rule
many skies.

Generic name:
Cathartes.

Purifier.
When they fly,

they soar
for hours,

riding high
thermals,

gliding
on bountiful

rivers of air.
Tippy in flight,

they balance
and right,

hover and crown.
Pacific

creatures,
catholic

in their taste
for carrion,

they do not fight
or kill their prey.

Their feet
are clawed,

but weak,
as are their beaks.

They are benign
and much maligned.

Glory Train

Cleaning
house,

I find, in
a dried-out

flower
of brown

froth,
the tiny

skeleton
of a bat.

I set it on
a white plate

and tweeze
debris

from its frame.
The hand-

wing bones
are thin

as veins —
a miracle

of design,
fine almost

to vanishing,
the ephemeral

on which
so much

depends.
The pelvis

is small
as a pushpin,

frailer than
eggshell;

the fragile
vestibule

of the ribs
is clean and

unbroken.
It harbors

eight
desiccated

larvae that had,
rather late,

hopped
aboard

this darkly
upholstered

glory train.
The minuscule

figure hints
at the beautiful

old rhyme
of moon

and ruin,
the darkness

in which
constellated

hungers twitch
and fly,

feed on each
other and die.

The Chickasaw Trees

are full of bees
the pretty white

panicles
everywhere

light
turn them

frantic
as they haul

their pollen
baskets

from star
to star

to fragrant
star this

industry
thrumming

in the hearts
of flatland

plums hums
in the lucky

air far
from where

war
goes on

and on and
here on

the sun-lit
prairie light

winds shift
and dusky

nouns are sung
from the trees

where an owl
frowns

in sleep
and later

comes
in the guise

of ghost
to say

he knows
that all

the people
in a world

without bees
are lost

Bird and Beast

Some say all birds are feather-brained,
Some say they're bright.
But I maintain that if you trained
your eye on, say, the Sandhill Crane,
you'd see that, feeding, or in flight,
he does not hedge or monetize,
unlike the master parasite,
who earth's demise
will underwrite.

Birding at the Hamilton County Phosphate Mines

The plunder
of the vast

pine woods
has sundered

earth's live
crust

from rock.
The earth

has been stripped
and flayed,

and great
white mounds

of chalky
phosphogypsum

loom, giant,
poisonous

breasts,
over milky

waste-clay
ponds. Here

thousands
and thousands

of birds
perch and swim,

dabble, soar,
and dive.

Hawk, duck,
stork, sora,

ahninga,
sparrow,

wren —
all thrive

in this
humming

mess.
Sorrow

yields
to dubious

wonder
at the fecund,

blowzy
zen.

The Truth About Cats

They kill
birds. As I

wish my
white cat

a Happy
New Year,

I see that
although

she heard
and flicked

an ear,
she cares

not a whit
for the tempo-

sphere,
that her map

of time
includes

simply here,
now,

the rhyme
of the cat food

can snapping
and the meat

in her mouth.
When her eyes

are fixed
on a bird,

her irises
dilate

so wide
it seems

the creature
might fly

right inside,
if it decided

to blow out
its own

little temporal
light in a flight

of featherweight
suicide.

Snowy Owl

A woman who looked like a snowy owl
knocked on my door last winter.
A bunch of artificial violets was pinned
to her gray woolen coat. She trudged through the snow

in high heels, sheathed in opaque plastic boots.
Her smile was bright as a blast furnace,
and her eyes, behind double-thick glasses,
brimmed over with inspiration. "Do you,"

she began, "ever think about living forever?"
"Sometimes," I replied, staring into her yellow eyes.
She then reached in her purse and pulled out a mouse
that swung from her gnarled and horny fingertips, dead.

"The gift of eternal life is not for mice.
It is for us, who know the beauty of death,
the light in the blood as it falls to earth.
Who know too the good liquor of loss,

blue terror in the fall from a great height.
Who know cruelty can be beautiful
and love a poor relation in this fine world full
of contradiction." After this she smiled

more brightly than ever and with great gentleness
and pride restored the dead mouse to her purse.

"Do you have any questions?" she inquired.
I thought for a moment and said, "yes,

are you partial to a gamy cassoulet?
Perhaps I could persuade you to step in for dinner?"
She puffed out her chest and glared. The violets shivered.
She then wheeled on a sharp heel and flew away.

Swan Lake

Calling on a lady who had no maid,
I was forced to furnish my own.
In fact, I took a tea-set and golden plate,
and peonies in a silver bowl.

"My word," I said to her on arriving,
"how those mourning doves do carry on!"
She peered at me most peculiarly
and ushered me into the atrium,

where scissor-tailed darts with silver spurs
and crescent wrens piped up in tandem.
She offered some crickets and Chinese tea
and we chirped through the hour most properly.

Then an odd thing transpired, direct après tea-time
(my girl had gathered the mother-of-pearl) —
my hostess, half-lidded, began to hum
a most remarkable tedium

that crept into my dangling ear-lobes,
a shell-pink delicto if I ever heard one:
I had me a paraquat once sung so pooty
I sold my soul to a sailor-man.

I had never heard so lovely a bird-song
and fell to my knees in a reverie,

when a ruby-throated swan approached me,
duplicitous heart, amour in his eye,

a glittering black pool of romance
in which I secretly longed to swim,
so after a spot of poetic reflection,
I removed my jewels and dove in.

Sparrowing

we fan
out in

a human
line and

scrabble
through

shrubs and
high grasses

and keep
our eyes

skint
for little

brown
explosions

which might
mean vesper

or grasshopper
savannah

or song
depending on

eye ring
or size

on brow
streaked

or unstreaked
on color

bright or
duller

and habit —
an Easter

egg hunt
for the grown

up set
a feast

of conundrum
sans rabbit

Bird Words

tanager
gnat-catcher

caspian tern
goat-sucker

chimney swift
canvasback

erne
bristle-thighed

curlew and
mandarin duck

fly like
the heartstrings

the stricken
and plucked

bunting
and oriole

veery
and lark

sing for
the deepest down

gold in the dark
godwit

and goldfinch
and stilt

on the fly
give me a gannet

to gladden
the eye

sora and
phalarope

phoebe
and kite

dicksissel
sapsucker

flicking
the night

magnificent
frigatebird

pinions
unfurled

the light
and the feathered

heart verbs
of the world

Blue

The great blue
song of the earth
is sung in all
the best venues —
treetop, marsh,
desert, shore —
and on this spring
day in the wetlands
where, under
a late sun,
we stand alone
and in love
with each other
and the passing day
we watch a cormorant
whose eye is ringed
in blue diamonds,
a shimmering lure,
and we love this blue
and this dark bird
and this deepening sky
that pinks and hums
in the west, and then

the bird opens his beak
and flutters his throat
and the late

afternoon light
illuminates
the inside tissue
of his mouth
which is as blue
as his ocular jewelry,
as blue as the bluest
ocean, as blue
as the sky in all
its depth, as blue
as the back of the small
and determined beetle
who struggles to roll
his enormous dung ball
in his own breeding bid
to enchant another
small blue miracle.

Osprey and Needlefish

The raptor
plunges

and clasps
in yellow talons

a thrashing
slender ribbon

of scale
and bone,

almost
too large

for its grasp.
They lisp

through
sunglare —

now up,
now down —

the fish
drowning

in air,
gasping

brute flesh,
until

the osprey
firms

control,
rights course,

the struggling
needlefish

a shuddering
keel

and they gain
altitude

and wheel
into the woods

where a brood
of wide-

mouthed heads
awaits

its lively
silver food

Loon

Designed
in cold

beautiful lines.
Brilliantined

black head,
fire-red eyes

that defy
the darkness

of the water
in which it thrives.

In pure lines
it dives

for lively
prey, lightning

in black,
as it sweeps

its waterways
with sharp eyes.

At home in deep
cold water,

at home in the dome
of the sky,

at home in flight
as it roams

from summer
to winter,

its unearthly cries
haunt our sleep.

They bring splinters
of wildness

to our nights
as we navigate

through dreams
and the streaming

wakes of the trails
we earthlings make.

Black-bellied Whistling Ducks

winter
in the wetland.

they chatter
and whistle

and clamor
and niggle

in the piccolo
language which

bristles
and gnaws

on the possibilities
and flaws

of the humid
moment. They rise

and scatter,
wheel and land

in hyacinth,
lotus, thistle,

draw and re-draw
the outlines

of their small,
liquid

societies.
Their sentences

are fatter
and wetter

than ours —
in ever-diminishing

spaces their patois
spins chords

on water,
sustenance,

mates,
and wind

in regal,
skittery notes

and then
an eagle

bears down
from a cloud

and the crowd
explodes —

a great swirl,
a gigantic

black and white
sneeze,

the sizzle, hiss,
and wheeze

of skirling,
feathered fright.

What Rough Beast

A thousand cranes
stutter and yak

on the distant mudflats
The prairie

is all watershine
and wind, riffle

and serpentine
trace

Spider works
laden with light

hang like handkerchiefs
in the high asters

This present
seems infinite

and intimate
and yet the spirit

anticipates
the odor of rain

and contemplates
disaster

Birding at the Dairy

We're searching
for the single

yellow-headed
blackbird

we've heard
commingles

with thousands
of starlings

and brown-headed
cowbirds,

when the many-
headed body

arises
and undulates,

a sudden congress
of wings

in a maneuvering
wave that veers

and wheels, a fleet
and schooling swarm

in synchronous alarm,
a bloom radiating

in ribbons, in sheets,
in waterfall,

a murmuration
of birds

that turns
liquid in air,

that whooshes
like waves

on the shore,
or the breath

of a great
seething prayer.

King Vulture

Sarcoramphus Papa

Everything dies. Nothing dies.
That's the story of the Book.

If the Book were a bird
Those two sentences
Would be its wings.

—Gregory Orr, from *Concerning the
Book that is the Body of the Beloved*

The smashed
carcass

of the small
deer in the road

is translated
into flight

in the body
of this bright-

faced purifier,
its purple shawl

of feathers
clashing

with the red,
orange, and blue

featherless head.
He frees a load

from its cache
of bone

and rises
with the freight

of flesh
and fur,

and turns
it into sky-

born word.

Thirty white

pelicans kettle
up in the sky

lazing in helical
praise of high

thermals which
hold them circling

pinned
to the pellicle

of blue film
between skin

and all things
angelical

Amazed

Today on
the windy

prairie
black clouds

sheet down
in the east

I'm going
to get wet

The blue-eyed
grass clumps

in tuffets
beside

the path
They startle

the corner
of the eye

like the swish
of an unseen

snake through
dry weeds

quick-turns
the head

A large
turtle naps

on the mud
bank

in the placid
shadow

of a torpid
alligator

It rains
a little

and I get
a little

wet with
the black-

necked stilts
who yap

like dogs
in swift

flight
over this

wet-bright
landscape

where
a single

whooping
crane slogs

in the shallow
marsh

hunting
for brunch

and thrusts
its fine red-

knotted
head into

the muck
and emerges

in black-face
and blinks

and we are
all amazed

Dry Season

The sky is full
of leaving cranes

in rafts
and wheels

in singletons
and vees

rattling
their leaving

song across
the spectacle

of spirits
in sunlight

They ride
the drafts

and spiral
up — a dry

symphony and
woody refrain

filling the clouds
with sonic grain

We wish them
safe passage

from the empty
fields we stand

in now,
as we fasten

our soul-belts
and pray

for rain

Witness Tree Junction, Rochelle, FL

We walk the dry path — it hasn't rained for months —
through pine stand, hammock, desiccated swamp.
The still-hot sun is veiled by merciful clouds.
Hundreds of robins flush — it's a sharp-shinned
hawk, while far from this transitive landscape
appalling darkness prepares for its pomp
and circumstances. There must be a map
in the lush, ever-vernal grace of language
that might help us emerge from the gloom,
though I can't hear it now. Old sounds: shrouded
whispers, in tongues, the hum between love
and the battered earth's bruised chorus.
A golden orb-weaver hangs in her loom
of evanescence and calmly observes us.

November 9, 2016

*

The Hard Saving

*—for the Conservation Stewards of the Alachua
Conservation Trust*

The sun hums low on a steaming river.
A late light whispers through littering oaks.
The long hours speak in the tongues of birds,
in the slip of leaves to the listening ground.

This earth-sprung language, bright and resonant,
rattles from the throats of the leaving cranes;
it springs from abundant shining waters
as they lunge for distant mangrove shores;

it pours in the dialect of thundering rain
which adds to the fund of the mother tongue,
the source that lies low, transparent and full,
the life-stream, the fundament, the great clear heart.

In full fine words the earth is speaking
to those who listen and care to respond.
But the subtle words are harder to hear
and harder to find and smaller. It's late.

Those who listen hear time stutter short,
hear squeals of profit shatter the peace.
The living words say *It's time, it's time,*
Put by the fragile growing treasure.

This saving is hard. There's hard labor in thrift.
But those who listen have been resourceful.
Some savings have accumulated and we are richer
for tenacious accounting of the living green.

We still have incomparable deep-voiced springs,
big river-making and brilliant sources,
tall grasses still whisper their shining songs,
dark nights are still lit by singing creatures.

Yet we must save more of our oldest reserve,
we must learn to balance trust and power;
we must sing the economy of saving grace,
we must continue that song and not stop saving.

Acknowledgments

These poems have previously been published in the following journals:

Academy of American Poets, *Poem-a-Day*
Alachua Conservation Trust Newsletter
American Journal of Poetry
The Arkansas International
Atlanta Review
Best American Poetry 2015
Bird Watcher's Digest
Birmingham Poetry Review
Blackbird
Cimarron Review
Dublin Poetry Review
Gavia: Tales from Loon Country
Gettysburg Review
Gulf Coast
Memorious
One
OnEarth
Plume
The Enchanting Verses
The Nation
The New Yorker

And I am more grateful than I can say to my poultry group and beloved friends and trusted readers: Geoff Brock, Joe Haldeman, Lola Haskins, Brandy Kershner, Michael Loughran, Randy Mann, and Lisa Zeidner. Thank you again and again and again and again.